Contents

Who were the Victorians?

The Victorians were the people who lived in Britain during the **reign** of Queen Victoria, from 1837 to 1901. During this time, the way people lived changed very quickly, and Britain became a world **superpower**.

From farming to factories

At the beginning of the Victorian age, most people lived in villages and worked on the land. By the end of the age, many people had moved into towns and cities. They worked there in factories, shops and offices. Factories made cheap **goods** in large quantities that were sold in Britain and in other countries. These huge changes are today known as the Industrial Revolution.

Victoria was only 18 years old when she became Queen of Great Britain and Ireland in 1838.

British colonies

Trading companies and the British army took over lands and countries around the world. These countries became **colonies** of the British **Empire**, and they supplied cheap foods such as tea and sugar and other materials the factories needed. This made Britain wealthier. Many individual people also became richer, and their lives improved, but others remained poor. The poorest people lived in streets of rundown buildings, called slums.

Victorian objects

A lot of **evidence** still exists from the Victorian period. Many of the magnificent public buildings, such as city halls, museums and railway stations, still stand in towns and city centres. The Victorians loved to collect things, such as fossils and paintings, which you can see in museums. They also wrote much about life at the time.

The Victorians invented the first postal service that used stamps to pay for a letter to be delivered. These 'penny reds' are some of the first stamps.

What does it tell us?

This painting from Victorian times shows a street filled with shops and shoppers. This tells us that the Victorians made, sold and bought many goods during this time.

The Industrial Revolution

The Industrial Revolution began about 100 years before Victoria was crowned, but it reached its height during Victorian times. Many factories were founded during this time and the railways were created.

Factories employed children as well as women to work the huge machines.

Factories

Before the Industrial Revolution, people spun **cotton** and wool and wove them into cloth on small machines in their homes. Then in the 1760s and 1770s new machines were invented that could spin and weave much faster. The machines were too big to fit into people's homes, so large factories were built to hold them. Factories produced huge amounts of cheap goods.

CHILD CHIMNEY SWEEPS

Many Victorian children had to work hard, sometimes in dangerous jobs. Some children were even made to climb inside large chimneys to clean the soot away.

What does it tell us?

This is a picture of Crystal Palace, built in 1851 to hold the Great Exhibition. It shows us that the Victorians were proud of their achievements. The goods that Britain made, such as china and steam engines, were displayed inside. **Exhibits** from other parts of the Empire included an elephant and a huge diamond from India.

Iron and steel

For centuries, people had known how to make iron from **iron ore**. They also knew that steel, made from iron, was stronger. In 1856, a new way of changing iron to steel was invented. As a result, large amounts of cheap steel could be produced. The Victorians used iron and steel to build bridges and railway tracks, and to make vehicles and machines.

✱ *Victorian ironworks used giant hammers powered by steam to hammer red-hot iron into shape. This steam hammer was at an ironworks in Manchester.*

Transport

New inventions totally changed the way people travelled and **transported** goods. Before trains, people travelled by horse or walked. Goods were carried by horse and cart, or on **barges** and boats along **canals** and rivers. These journeys were usually slow and difficult. Most people stayed in the same village all their lives.

Steam engines

The first steam locomotives pulled wagons of coal and iron, but in 1825 the first passenger train puffed for 9 miles (14 kilometres) between Stockton and Darlington in north-east England. By the end of Queen Victoria's reign, railway lines linked every town and city and also many villages. Ships with steam engines began to take over from sailing ships.

🏭 Building railway lines was a huge and often dangerous task. Railway workers, on very low pay, blasted tunnels through hillsides and built bridges across valleys.

NO TOILETS!

Although train journeys could take all day, there were no toilets on board the train. Passengers had to dash out at stations along the way.

Bicycles and cars

Pedal bicycles were invented in France in 1861 and soon came to Britain. Women as well as men rode them. The first car that used a petrol engine was invented in Germany in 1885, but early cars were too expensive for ordinary people to buy.

✳ *The first cars were often called 'horseless carriages'. They looked like a horse-drawn carriage, except they had an engine instead of a horse.*

What does it tell us?

Bicycles with large front wheels and a small back wheel were called penny-farthings after the large penny and small farthing coins. They became popular in the 1870s. The pedals were attached to the front wheel and they were difficult to ride. But the larger the front wheel, the faster the bicycle could go!

The growth of cities

Cities grew fast during the 19th century. In 1801, 75,000 people lived in Manchester – by 1901 there were 654,000. There were two reasons for the increase. Thousands of people left the countryside and moved to towns and cities to find work. And the whole population of Britain increased, as families became larger.

Slums

People who came to the cities often lived in crowded slums, where disease was common. The houses were built close together, and large families might live in just one room, with little or no furniture. In the 1840s however, **reformers** persuaded Parliament to pass laws that helped to improve the lives of slum-dwellers.

Many people who lived in the countryside were also very poor. This engraving of the inside of a farm labourer's cottage in Dorset was drawn in 1846.

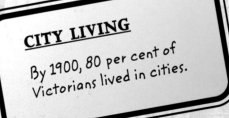

CITY LIVING
By 1900, 80 per cent of Victorians lived in cities.

What does it tell us?

The poorest Victorians who had no work and no money might be sent to live and work in a **workhouse**. Here, conditions were very harsh and people could be punished for minor offences, such as swearing. The punishments included beatings and being given even less food than usual. This picture shows a Victorian workhouse.

Dangerous streets

Even after the slums were improved, the streets were still dangerous. They were badly lit, so **pickpockets** and other **criminals** found it easy to rob passers-by. Charles Dickens's novel called *Oliver Twist*, described how children were employed by criminals to pick the pockets of wealthy people.

An artist's engraving of Manchester in about 1850. Rows of houses were built close to factories, which filled the air with black smoke.

Houses and homes

As the Industrial Revolution and the Empire made people richer, many Victorians were able to afford comfortable homes. Their houses were often built in rows joined side by side. They were known as terraces and had a garden at the back.

Victorian houses

Today many families still live in Victorian houses. Although they look much the same on the outside they are quite different inside. Victorians had no central heating, no refrigerators, vacuum cleaners or automatic washing machines. They crammed their rooms with lots of heavy furniture, pictures, plates and ornaments.

THE NEW "CARRON" RANGE

The Latest in Cooking Ranges.

The "CARRON" RANGE with the inner GLASS OVEN DOOR, which enables the cook to watch the progress of cooking without interfering with the uniform temperature of oven. The Thermometer attached ensures perfect heat regulation.

The range that effects the greatest economy, and gives the best results.

Fire can be increased or diminished at will, by lowering or raising bottom-grate.

The flues are formed in Cast iron, thus obviating the expense of constructing brick flues, which are invariably unsatisfactory.

A perfect boiler system gives ample supply of hot water. Boiler can be taken out without removing Range.

The heat can be regulated by means of conveniently placed indicating dampers.

A cast-steel hinged folding-down front grate enables the fire chamber to be cleaned with ease.

The new "CARRON" is undoubtedly the most artistic and serviceable Range on the market. CALL AND INSPECT.

No. 51 Descriptive Range pamphlet on application to—

CARRON COMPANY
INCORPORATED BY ROYAL CHARTER 1773

CARRON, Stirlingshire.

Also at Phœnix Foundry, Sheffield.

A complete assortment of CARRON manufactures on view at the Company's Showrooms :— London (City) 15, Upper Thames St., E.C.; (West End) 23, Princes St., Cavendish Sq., W., 3, Berners St., W.; Liverpool—22 ¾, Red Cross St.; Glasgow—125, Buchanan St.; Edinburgh —114, George St.; Manchester—24, Brazennose St.; Bristol—6, Victoria St.; Newcastle-on-Tyne—13, Prudhoe St.; Birmingham—218, 220, 222, Corporation St.; Dublin—44, Grafton St

❋ New household equipment, such as this 'Carron' oven range, improved life in wealthier Victorian houses.

INDIVIDUAL SHOPS

Victorians ate mostly fresh food, which they usually bought from many different shops. There were no supermarkets. Instead different shops sold groceries, fish, bread and meat.

Servants

Victorians thought that it was very important to keep their homes clean and tidy. Almost everything had to be done by hand, but most families, except the poorest, had at least one servant. Servants worked long hours. They would get up early to light the fires, and they kept everything clean and polished. People from poor families often became servants when they were still children.

⊗ Mrs Beeton's Everyday Cookery and Housekeeping Book *was a huge success. It taught women how to cook, and also how to run their homes.*

What does it tell us?

Kitchen maids used this machine (below) to clean knives. Before stainless steel was invented, knives often became stained and rusty. The maid put the knives in the slots and then added special powder. As she turned the handle brushes inside the machine cleaned and polished the knives.

15

Inventions and discoveries

In 1831, just before Queen Victoria came to the throne, Michael Faraday discovered how to produce electricity. His discovery led to the invention of telephones, electric lights and many other electrical **devices**.

Instant messages

In 1837 a **telegraph** wire was set up in London. The telegraph used a code called Morse code to send messages instantly from one place to another. Then in 1876, Alexander Graham Bell invented the telephone. For the first time, people many miles apart could speak to each other.

MURDERER CAUGHT!

An escaping murderer, John Tawell, caught the 7.42 train from Slough to London. The Slough police 'telegraphed' the London police, who then waited to meet the train and caught him!

✵ *The first phones did not have numbers to dial. Instead the caller lifted the receiver and turned the handle. An operator then asked them which number they wanted to call.*

Lighting

For most of the period, people lit their homes using gas lamps, oil lamps or candles, but these lights produced smoke and soot. The first 'clean' electric light bulbs were invented in 1879.

A revolutionary idea

In 1831, Charles Darwin sailed around the world examining and collecting different species (kinds) of plants and animals. In 1859, he shocked the world when he published his theory of evolution. It said that each species was not separately created, but had evolved from an earlier, slightly different species.

Charles Darwin lived from 1809 until 1882. His theory of evolution explains why there are such a great variety of plants and animals on Earth.

What does it tell us?

The first cameras needed several seconds to take a photograph. This meant that the subjects had to keep perfectly still. The Victorians were the first people to take photographs that they could print and keep. They show us how people lived then.

Fashion and culture

Strict rules controlled how people dressed and behaved in every situation. Women, for example, might wear different clothes in the morning, afternoon and evening. Men also dressed **formally**. They often wore top hats, ties and suits with waistcoats, and carried a **cane**.

✷ *The man in this Victorian photograph is dressed formally in a shirt, tie and a suit with a waistcoat.*

✷ *Poor and working people wore hard-wearing practical clothes. Children and women wore aprons.*

What does it tell us?

Women did not dress for comfort during Victorian times. They wore tight structures under their dresses called **corsets**. These covered their chest and waist and could make breathing difficult. Women also wore a stiff shaped frame called a bustle beneath their dresses (right). This was a wire cage that held a dress out at the back.

Petticoats and corsets

In the first half of Queen Victoria's reign, women wore many layers of **petticoats** under their skirts. They used corsets that were tied tightly to make their waists look slim. Some doctors worried that they were bad for the women's health, because they made it difficult to breathe.

Crinolines and bustles

Fashions changed in the later part of Victoria's life. Petticoats were replaced by a light wire cage, called a crinoline, which held the skirt out all around. Later, the crinoline was replaced by the bustle, worn at the back. Fashionable dresses were then flat at the front and full at the back.

PIANO PETTICOATS

The Victorians thought that legs should be covered at all times. They even made petticoats for piano legs!

victorian families

Most Victorians had large families. After Queen Victoria married Prince Albert, she had nine children. Some families had many more. Life for most women centred around their families.

Work and marriage

In poor families, everyone had to work, including the children. Women worked in factories and did whatever jobs they could to keep their families out of the workhouse. Young girls from poor families often became servants.

Better off women did not work, and many could afford to pay nurses and **governesses** to look after their children for them.

This family photo of a mother with her four daughters was taken in Birmingham in about 1880. Children were meant to be loving and dutiful.

New jobs for women

As time moved on, more jobs became available to young women. Previously, poor, but educated, women became governesses who taught children at home. Now many began to work in offices, or in new, large **department stores**. Once they married, however, they had to give up working. Their job was to bring up a family of children.

Women were not allowed to **vote** during Victorian times. This painting shows a woman speaking about women's rights at a public gathering.

WOMEN REBEL

Women had no control of their lives — they couldn't even vote. Some women began to demand more rights. They wanted to go to university, like their brothers.

What does it tell us?

This statue of an angel comes from a Victorian grave in London. It probably marks the grave of a child or a mother, who may have died in childbirth. Infant death and death in childbirth were common in Victorian families.

Victorian children

Victorian children were treated strictly. Adults expected them to be 'seen but not heard'. In richer families, children lived in rooms at the top of the house. Here small children were cared for by **nursemaids**, and older children were taught at home by a governess or tutor. However, as time went on, more and more Victorian children went to school.

Children played with lots of toys, including dolls and doll houses, puzzles and toy animals.

What does it tell us?

This Victorian jigsaw puzzle consists of wooden cubes with part of a picture stuck on the sides of each cube. When you arrange them in the right order they make six different pictures. Each one shows a scene from the Bible. The puzzle tells us that Victorians wanted children to learn as they played and to follow the teachings of the Bible.

Poor children

Poor children, some as young as five years old, were forced to work to earn money that their families desperately needed. In 1842 the government passed laws to prevent children younger than ten from working in coalmines. Two years later, laws limited the number of hours children could work. Later laws said that all children had to go to school for some hours, but many parents could not afford the penny a week that school cost.

Schools

The author Charles Dickens wrote a novel called *Hard Times*, published in 1854. It described a school in which pupils learned lots of facts but were not allowed to use their imaginations. Schools gradually improved, and in 1891, they became free for everyone. New schools were built in every town, and many of them are still used today.

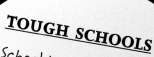

TOUGH SCHOOLS

School teachers were very strict. They used leather straps or canes to punish children. They were punished for talking, being late, and also for just being slow to learn.

This photo shows a Victorian classroom. The lessons for the day are written on the blackboard. The teacher's cane lies ready on his desk.

Entertainment

As working conditions improved, people had more time off. With better pay, they could afford to enjoy themselves. Sports, such as football, cricket and rugby became popular. People played sports themselves and followed their local team.

Activities for everyone

Many kinds of public entertainment began during the Victorian age. Parks and gardens were set aside for the public, and museums, art galleries and public libraries were opened in towns and cities. Circuses and fairs toured the country, and drew in huge crowds of people. The railways made it easier for people to get out of the towns and cities. In the summer, families flocked to the seaside. Often it was just for the day, but sometimes for a week's holiday.

Victorian fairs, such as the one shown in this photograph, were popular. Acts included tight-rope walkers and jugglers.

What does it tell us?

Victorians of all ages enjoyed themselves at the seaside. As this picture shows, most people did not take off their clothes – they even kept their hats and boots on! Some people did swim in the sea, but first they put on swimming costumes that covered their whole bodies. This seaside town has two piers, built out over the sea, for people to walk along.

Home entertainment

At home, families amused themselves together. Almost everyone could play the piano and the whole family would gather round to sing popular songs. Family games, such as charades and hunt the thimble, were popular, especially at Christmas. Quieter entertainment included reading aloud, embroidery and card games, such as **patience**.

CHRISTMAS TRADITIONS

Many of our Christmas traditions began during the Victorian age. These include decorated Christmas trees and making Christmas cards.

✳ *These Victorian Christmas cards show images of Christmas, including Father Christmas and sleeping children waiting for him to bring their presents.*

Quiz

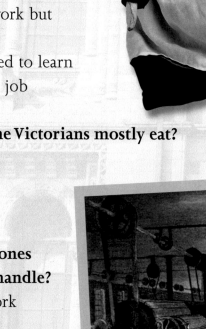

1. **What was The Great Exhibition?**
   a. A large dolls' house used
      by Queen Victoria
   b. The first indoor ice rink
   c. An exhibition of goods
      made in Britain

2. **How did people travel before
   railways were invented?**
   a. By plane
   b. By horse
   c. By car

3. **Who were sent to live in a workhouse?**
   a. People who were out of work and
      had nowhere to live
   b. People who wanted to work but
      could not find a job
   c. Young people who needed to learn
      a skill to help them get a job

4. **Which kind of food did the Victorians mostly eat?**
   a. Dried food
   b. Frozen food
   c. Fresh food

5. **Why did early first telephones
   have to be wound with a handle?**
   a. To make the machine work
   b. To get the attention of
      the operator
   c. To ring the bell of the telephone
      that was being called

6. **What was a bustle?**
   a. A kind of cap that covered a woman's hair
   b. A kind of carriage drawn by horses
   c. A wire cage that a woman wore over her bottom

7. **What was Charles Dickens' novel called?**
   a. Hard Luck
   b. Hard Times
   c. Hard Years

8. **What were women expected to do after they married?**
   a. Leave their job and look after their families
   b. Clean their home every day
   c. Work fewer hours at their jobs

9. **From what age were children allowed to work before 1842?**
   a. The age of 15
   b. The age of 10
   c. The age of 5

10. **Which of these were invented during Victorian times?**
    a. The steam engine
    b. The bicycle
    c. The first aeroplane that flew

ANSWERS

1c   6c
7b   8a
2b   9b
3a   10b
4c
5b

Timeline

1776	James Watt's steam engine first used.
1825	The first passenger railway ran between Stockton and Darlington in north-east England.
1831	Michael Faraday invented the first dynamo – a machine that generated electric current.
1837	Princess Victoria became queen of Britain at 18 years old and the Victorian age began.
1838	Coronation of Queen Victoria.
1839	William Henry Fox Talbot, who invented taking photographs using negative paper, showed his photographic prints to the Royal Society.
1840	Queen Victoria married Prince Albert.
1842	Parliament made it illegal for children under the age of 10 and women to work underground in a coalmine.
1844	Parliament stopped children between the ages of 8 and 12 from working more than 6.5 hours a day.
1851	The Great Exhibition was held at the Crystal Palace in London.
1853–56	France, Britain, Turkey and Sardinia fought against Russia in the Crimean War.
1859	Charles Darwin published *On the Origin of Species*, which described his theory of evolution.
1861	Prince Albert died and Queen Victoria went into mourning. Pedal bicycles were invented in France.
1870	Board schools opened to provide education for all 5 to 13 year-old children.
1874	Parliament made it illegal to force workers to work more than 10 hours a day or to employ children under the age of 14.
1876	Alexander Graham Bell invented the first telephone.
1879	The first electric light bulbs were invented.
1880	All children up to the age of 10 had to go to school.
1891	Schools were made free for all children between the ages of 5 and 13.
1892	Twelve football teams formed the First Division.
1901	Queen Victoria died.

Glossary

barge A boat with a flat bottom, used for carrying goods.

canal A special waterway for boats to move from one place to another.

cane A long stick used by someone to help them walk or to beat someone.

colonies Countries conquered and ruled by another country.

corset Underwear with strings pulled tight to make the waist look smaller.

cotton Thread or material made from the fluffy seed heads of the cotton plant.

criminal Someone who has done something that is forbidden by law.

department store A large shop that sells many different things.

device A gadget or machine that is designed to do something in particular.

empire All the countries or areas of land controlled by one country.

evidence Objects, such as clothes or toys, that show the facts of a situation.

exhibit Something that is displayed to people in, for example, an exhibition.

formally Something done according to set rules or manners.

goods Things that are bought and sold.

governess A woman who teaches children in their home.

iron ore A substance found in the ground from which the metal iron is made.

nursemaid Someone who looks after young children, also called a nanny.

patience A game of cards for one person.

petticoat An underskirt made up of layers of fabric and worn beneath dresses.

pickpocket A criminal who steals money and valuables from people's pockets.

reformers People who wanted to make life fairer for everyone.

reign A period of time that a king or queen rules.

superpower A country that has great wealth and power in the world.

telegraph A way of sending messages along an electricity wire using a code of dots and dashes.

trading companies Companies that buy and sell goods.

transported Something or someone carried from one place to another.

vote To take part in an election.

workhouse A building in which poor people lived and worked for free.

Index

History From Objects

Contents of titles in the series:

WAYLAND